THE LITTLE BOOK OF

RANCH
Dressing

Published in 2022 by OH!
An Imprint of Welbeck Non-Fiction Limited,
part of Welbeck Publishing Group.
Based in London and Sydney.
www.welbeckpublishing.com

Disclaimer: This book is intended for general informational purposes only and should not be relied upon as recommending or promoting any specific practice, diet or method of treatment. It is not intended to diagnose, advise, treat or prevent any illness or condition and is not a substitute for advice from a professional practitioner of the subject matter contained in this book. You should not use the information in this book as a substitute for medication, nutritional, diet, spiritual or other treatment that is prescribed by your practitioner. The publisher makes no representations or warranties with respect to the accuracy, completeness or currency of the contents of this work, and specifically disclaim, without limitation, any implied warranties of merchantability or fitness for a particular purpose and any injury, illness, damage, death, liability or loss incurred, directly or indirectly from the use or application of any of the contents of this book. Furthermore, the publisher is not affiliated with and does not sponsor or endorse any uses of or beliefs about in any way referred in this book.

ISBN 978-1-83861-087-6

Compilation and editorial: Theresa Bebbington and Katie Hewett
Associate Publisher: Lisa Dyer
Design: Lucy Palmer
Production: Felicity Awdry

A CIP catalogue record for this book is available from the British Library

Printed in Dubai

10 9 8 7 6 5 4 3 2 1

Illustrations: Shutterstock.com

★ ★ ★

THE LITTLE BOOK OF

RANCH

Dressing

AN HOMAGE TO THE CULT CLASSIC

THAT MAKES EVERYTHING BETTER

OH!

Contents

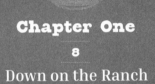

Introduction

The best-selling salad dressing in the U.S. since 1992 with more sales than ketchup, the condiment the *Washington Post* called "extravagant and trashy" may not be fine dining but it sure is versatile. A celebration of this food favorite—with fun facts, celebrity quotes, snappy slogans, and over 50 recipes—this little book is your gateway to life on the ranch. Here you will learn to make it from scratch, fold it into comforting snacks, conjure up tasty dips, and use it for brunch, lunch, supper, picnics, and game day snacking. It's definitely not just for salads.

Discover the cowboy origins of this creamy concoction in the first chapter, Down on the Ranch, and how this once-obscure salad dressing evolved from a small home-based business to global domination.

The second chapter, Dip It, Dunk It, Dress It, offers recipes for dressings, dips, and sauces with ideas on its many accompaniments, from crispy tortillas to barbecued wings. The secret ingredients that make ranch ranch are revealed, along with a range of variations and takes on the classic buttermilk style. A basic creamy recipe is given on page 44 with the dried seasoning mix supplied on page 56, and either of these homemade versions or any commercial store-bought alternative can be used in the recipes that call for them throughout the book.

Chapter three, Snacks, Salads, & Sides, and chapter four, Hearty Helpings, are packed with recipes, ideas, and food hacks for everything from crunchy ranch-flavored pretzels, coleslaw, and green beans, to mac-and-cheese and marinades.

Because it's the condiment that people put on everything, from chicken nuggets to cereal, try some of the more unusual and exotic sweet and savory pairings—tried and tested, loved and loathed—from chapter five, Ranch & . . .

And finally, if you're totally obsessed with ranch, and of course you are, realize you are not alone. Chapter six, The Ranch Fan Club, is devoted to extolling the virtues of this cult classic and tracing its cameo appearances in TV, in the movies, and on social media. Of course, you're a bonafide member already.

Chapter One

Down on the Ranch

Discover the entrepreneurial origins of America's favorite dressing, along with entertaining anecdotes and fun facts.

Henson's Hidden Valley

Ranch as we know it was first created in 1948
by plumber-turned-cowboy Steve Henson,
who started out serving his dressing to fellow
workers during a stint as a construction worker
and sometime cook in Anchorage, Alaska.
When he moved to his Californian dude ranch,
Hidden Valley, in 1956, he served the dressing to
customers at his ranch kitchen, and by 1959, his
make-at-home packet mix was being sold for
75 cents via mail order. Popularity soared, the
company was bought by Clorox for $8 million in
1972, with Cool Ranch Doritos launching in 1987,
Ranch Wavy Lay's potato chips in 1994, and the
rest is history . . .

Twisted Ranch

The restaurant **Twisted Ranch** in St. Louis, Missouri, was founded on a passionate love for ranch dressing. Their motto is that

nothing is "un-ranchable."

Not only does the restaurant use ranch as a prominent component in every dish on the menu, but it produces over 33 house-made varieties of the dressing, all made fresh daily. And yes, it even makes desserts, such as bread pudding , and cocktails with the classic house style. Why not try their **Twisted Mary** with ranch vodka in a ranch-seasoned rimmed glass?

Sweetwater Ranch

When the Hensons purchased the 120-acre ranch, first called Sweetwater, in San Marcos Pass, which can be found in the Santa Ynez Mountains outside of Santa Barbara, they offered their guests a place to go horseback riding, fishing, and hiking. But that wasn't the only experience the guests would have. The ranch kitchen was dishing up home-cooked meals with the tangy salad dressing Steve had created in Alaska.

What *IS* a Dude Ranch?

The best way of describing a dude ranch is that it's like an original Western all-inclusive vacation where you might encounter cattle work, horseback riding, or other outdoor experiences. Dude ranches were first established in the late nineteenth century for people from the Midwest and East Coast who wanted to rejuvenate their spirits and have a break from their hectic suburban lives.

"

If you wear cowboy or cowgirl clothes, are you ranch dressing?

"

A Piece of the Ranch

Steve Henson's guests must have given him positive feedback on the dressing because he soon was giving them bottles to take home with them. One day Henson mixed a batch for his friend Audrey Ovington, who owned Cold Spring Tavern. After tasting the dressing, Ovington was soon serving it to his customers, too.

B-ranching Out

It was only a matter of time before
Henson's ranch dressing would become
a commercial venture. In 1957, within a
few of years of buying the ranch, Henson
was selling packets of his dressing mix to
Kelley's Korner, a local store. The store
soon found the packets flying off the
shelves, with more than 140 packets being
sold in a two-day period.

No Room for Guests

Henson recognized that he had hit on something that would do well and soon the entrepreneur expanded into a mail-order business. Although it was now the mid 1960s and only about a decade since purchasing Hidden Valley Ranch, the dude ranch experience hadn't been a financial success, and Henson decided that it would no longer be open to guests.

BY MAIL ORDER

Henson's mail-order business was doing so well that the packets of dry ranch dressing mix gradually took over every room in the family's home. Each packet included a handwritten note to give directions on how to use the mix. **The Hensons were soon filling orders from all of the 50 states by the late 1960s, as well as taking orders for the packets from more than 30 countries.**

The Ranch Man

If you want to sell a product successfully, it's usually a good idea to establish a logo, and needless to say that would apply to Henson's ranch dressing. The packets were designed with a logo of the "Ranch man," a dancing cowboy near a fence, supposedly created by John Bersman—a cartoonist responsible for *The Flintstones*.

PACKING THE PACKETS

At first, Hidden Valley arranged for the packets of the dry dressing mix to be blended at Griffith Laboratories based in San Jose, and from there the mix would be shipped to a facility based in Los Angeles, where they could pack

35,000 packets
every 8 hours.

Colorado and Nevada would later become locations for making the condiment.

A Factory Opens

By the early 1970s, having outgrown the family ranch, the first factory for making ranch dressing opened, allowing for a much greater volume of production, enough to be distributed to supermarkets in the Southwest. Not only that, but Henson's ranch would become the newly incorporated Hidden Valley Ranch Food Products, Inc. headquarters.

What Makes a Dressing a Ranch Dressing?

America's favorite salad dressing uses flavorings similar to other dressings, such as salt, garlic, onion, spices, and herbs mixed into a liquid base. In the case of ranch, that base is mayonnaise or another type of oil emulsion, but the main ingredient—buttermilk—is what makes this dressing the star.

What's in a Name?

In a bid to compete with Hidden Valley Ranch's popular dressing, Kraft Foods and General Foods both introduced their own versions of dry seasoning packets, but labeled them "ranch style." They were both sued for trademark infringement in one particular case—not by Hidden Valley Ranch (although they were suing General Foods at the time in a separate case), but by Waples-Platter Companies, a Texas-based business with no interest in ranch dressing but the manufacturer of Ranch Style Beans. The judge ruled in favor of Waples-Platter, noting there was no competition between it and Hidden Valley Ranch.

Reformulated Ingredients

When Clorox—the company behind household cleaning products, such as Pine-Sol—took over the Hidden Valley Ranch brand in 1972, they decided to change the dressing to make it more convenient for consumers. At the time, the packet ingredients had to be mixed with both mayonnaise and buttermilk, but few people kept the more costly buttermilk in the refrigerator. So buttermilk flavoring was added to the mix, which meant that ordinary milk could be used instead.

NO FRIDGE NEEDED

Clorox continued to tinker with the ingredients used in the Hidden Valley Ranch brand and came up with a new formulation in 1983 that meant ranch dressing in the bottle no longer had to be stored in the refrigerator. Not surprisingly, the popularity of the dressing soared, with the product available in both packet and bottle versions.

Shelf Life

Because ranch dressing has a high dairy content, which normally spoils quickly, it presented Clorox's team with a real challenge. They needed to come up with a blend of preservatives that would work without noticeably altering the taste. The developers managed to do this, giving their ranch dressing a shelf life of about 150 days—but they kept their formula a secret. However, it's reasonable to guess that calcium disodium ethylenediaminetetraacetate wasn't one of Henson's ingredients.

Ranch v. the Others

By the mid 1980s, it was increasingly more common to find all types of salad dressings in "shelf stable" bottles in the supermarket.

But why was ranch dressing becoming so popular?

Let's compare it to other dressings: It lacks the chili sauce that is an important ingredient in Thousand Island and it doesn't have the anchovies found in Caesar and Green Goddess dressings, which put off some people. And Italian dressing, which is mostly herbs in a vinaigrette, doesn't sate the appetite of those wanting something a little creamier but not as fatty as mayonnaise.

BETTER FOR BREAD

By the late 1980s, ranch dressing was making its way into the fast-food chains and other casual-dining establishments, which were finding that the dressing was ideal for spreading on burgers and sandwiches. It posed a few advantages over other condiments: Mayonnaise has a thick texture that some customers found undesirable, while oil-and-vinegar dressings seep into bread, making it soggy.

But Is It Good for You?

Ever wondered if there's anything of nutritional benefit in ranch dressing?

One tablespoon of the creamy condiment will provide you with 18.8 mcg of vitamin K, almost one-quarter of your total daily needs, as well as smaller quantities of vitamin E and phosphorus.

However, only one tablespoon of the dressing also has 72.6 calories and 7.7 grams total fat (12 percent of the recommended daily limits). And that's only one tablespoon.

The Competition

By the late 1980s, a number of other manufacturers were getting in on the act. Because recipes cannot be patented, Clorox couldn't stop other companies, such as Kraft and Unilever (the latter is the owner of the Wish-Bone brand), from making their own ranch dressings. Nor could they be stopped from adding the flavor to an increasing range of snacks filling supermarket shelves, such as Cool Ranch Doritos, which first appeared in 1987.

ON THE FAST TRACK

The 1990s saw ranch dressing becoming a condiment of choice in even more fast-food establishments. It found its way into a number of products as the ideal moistening agent, such as in KFC's Twisters. But flavor also had a role to play, too. Applebee's Tequila Lime Chicken is coated in their "Mexi-ranch," and Chili's combined it with heat in their chipotle-flavored ranch.

Partnerships

Clorox didn't rest on its laurels with the success of their salad dressing. Taking a hint from the popularity of the Cool Ranch Doritos, they entered into a partnership with its creator, the potato chip manufacturer Frito-Lay. The two companies released their new product, Hidden Valley Ranch Wavy Lay's, in 1994.

21St-Century Trends

Executives of fast-food chains have kept an eye on their customers' appetite for the dressing. After learning that teenagers were dipping their pizza into ranch dressing,

Pizza Hut franchises in the South began selling their pies with a cup of ranch dressing.

They now offer Dippin' Strips Pizza, with pizza already cut into pieces for dipping, served with a ranch "sauce."

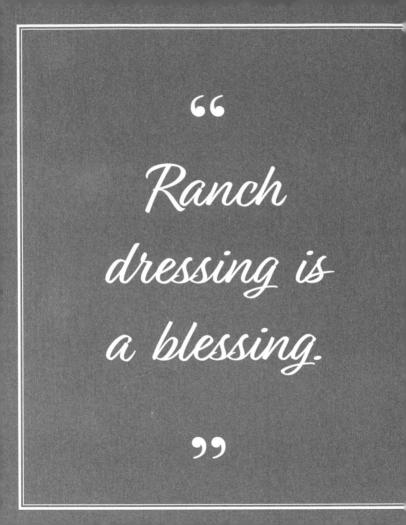

"

Ranch
dressing is
a blessing.

"

Variety Is the Spice of Life

Since Steve Henson first creation, Hidden Valley Ranch has developed more than 70 different varieties of its ranch dressing. His original is still the most popular, but new favorites include Cucumber Ranch and Bacon Ranch. And keeping up with the times, there's also a Vegan Ranch.

Chapter Two

Dip It, Dunk It, Dress It

Any way you serve it, ranch is delicious. Here are homemade recipes with variations that include cool cucumber, avocado, blue, plus ranchamole and ranch hummus.

What Makes Ranch Ranch?

The core ingredients of a good ranch must contain buttermilk, mayo, sour cream, onion and garlic powders, and plenty of dill, parsley, and chives.

It's a combination of creaminess and herbaceousness, with an undercurrent of onion and garlic and a hit of black pepper.

Buttermilk: Traditionally the fermented liquid leftover after churning cream into butter, buttermilk today is usually made from milk with added lactic bacteria. Giving the distinctive tangy taste to ranch, the dressing can't be made without it. Buttermilk is also high in vitamins, potassium, and calcium and is lower in fat than milk; the fermentation aids digestion and buttermilk has more calcium than regular milk. It yields a better flavor, better rise, and better texture in baked goods and can also be used to marinate meat.

Buttermilk substitute: If you don't have access to fresh buttermilk, you can use buttermilk powder prepared according to packet directions. Or make "sour milk" by mixing 1 tablespoon of lemon juice or vinegar to 1 cup milk. Let it rest for 5–10 minutes before using. If using vinegar, choose a clear variety, such as plain distilled, apple cider, rice, or Champagne vinegar.

Mayonnaise: Mayo adds thickness but it needs to be combined with sour cream to make the dressing extra creamy and lighten the dressing up. For a scoopable ranch dip, substitute more mayo and sour cream for the buttermilk; Greek yogurt and cream cheese are also common additions.

Spices: Essential are garlic power, onion powder, salt, and pepper. This is one of those cases when the dried version of garlic is so much better than fresh.

Herbs: Use chopped fresh dill, parsley, and chives, which enhance the oniony flavor. Dried can be substituted (at ⅓ the amount of fresh) but is best reserved for making a dry ranch spice mixture (see page 56).

Eat More Ranch

There are endless possibilities of accompaniments to ranch so the world is your oyster. Although anything crunchy or fried works well, happily there are healthy alternatives, too. Here are 20 popular dipping and dunking choices.

 Veggie sticks: carrots, cucumber, celery, bell pepper

 Roasted vegetables

 Whole raw veggies: mushrooms, cherry tomatoes, snap peas, broccoli and cauliflower florets

 Fruit slices: apple, orange, and pear

 Breadsticks or crackers

 Boiled baby potatoes

 Chicken wings

8 Chicken nuggets

 9 Mini hot dogs or sausages

 10 Pizza

 11 Fries: potato, sweet potato, or zucchini (courgette)

 12 Deep-fried pickles

 13 Battered onion rings

 14 Potato skins

 15 Jalapeño peppers

 16 Mozzarella sticks

 17 Tortilla chips

 18 Potato chips (crisps)

 19 Pretzels

 20 Tater tots

Homemade Ranch Dressing

Extra creamy, packed with herbs, and perfect for tossing with salad or used as a dipping sauce. **Makes about 2½ cups.**

½ cup plus 2 tablespoons mayonnaise
½ cup sour cream
½ cup buttermilk
1 tablespoon fresh lemon juice or white wine vinegar
1 teaspoon Worcestershire sauce
¼ cup chopped fresh dill
¼ cup chopped fresh flat-leaf parsley
¼ cup chopped fresh chives
½ teaspoon onion powder
½ teaspoon garlic powder
¼ teaspoon sea salt
¼ teaspoon freshly ground black pepper

In a medium bowl, combine the mayonnaise, sour cream, buttermilk, lemon juice or vinegar, and Worcestershire sauce. Stir until well blended and creamy. Add the herbs, onion and garlic powder, and salt and pepper. Taste and adjust seasonings. Refrigerate for 30 minutes before serving to allow the flavors to develop. Store, covered, in the fridge for 3–4 days.

Extra Garlicky Ranch

This is especially tasty with roasted vegetables, potatoes, and grilled and barbecued meat. **Makes about 3 cups.**

1 cup sour cream
1 cup mayonnaise
2 tablespoons dried dill
2 tablespoons chopped fresh parsley
2 tablespoons chopped fresh chives
1 tablespoon finely minced garlic
¾ cup buttermilk
Sea salt and pepper, to taste

Whisk the first six ingredients together until well blended. Slowly add the buttermilk, whisking constantly, to emulsify the dressing and get the desired consistency. Add a little more buttermilk for a thinner dressing and a little less for a thicker version. Season with salt and pepper to taste, and refrigerate for 30 minutes to allow the flavors to develop. Store, covered, in the refrigerator for 3–4 days.

Homemade Ranch Dip

This dip is thicker version of the dressing, which allows it to cling to crudités or chicken wings. It omits the buttermilk. **Makes about 2 cups.**

1 cup sour cream
1 cup mayonnaise
3 teaspoons freshly squeezed lemon juice
½ teaspoon dried dill
½ teaspoon dried chives
½ teaspoon dried parsley
½ teaspoon garlic powder
½ teaspoon onion powder
Sea salt and freshly ground black pepper
Chopped fresh chives, to garnish

Combine all of the ingredients except the fresh chives in a small bowl and whisk to combine. Cover and refrigerate for at least 1 hour to allow the flavors to develop. Sprinkle over the chives before serving.

Change up Your Dressing or Dip

Add Dijon mustard—great for hotdogs!

•

Crumble in bacon.

•

Add finely chopped chilies, sriracha,
or hot pepper sauce.

•

Make it smoky with chipotle (adobo) sauce.

•

Add in parmesan or cheddar cheese.

•

A pinch of cayenne and cumin
will give it a Southwestern twist.

•

Oregano instead of dill will give it an Italian flavor.

•

Add tahini for a sesame taste that's great on
sandwiches, salads, and with falafel.

Pesto Ranch Dip

Mix this into cold pasta salads, spoon over hot baked jacket potatoes, or use as a dip for veggies and crackers. **Makes about 1 cup.**

¼ cup mayonnaise
¼ cup Greek yogurt
2 tablespoons buttermilk
2 tablespoons basil pesto
1 tablespoon chopped fresh parsley
1½ teaspoons chopped fresh dill
½ teaspoon minced garlic
1 teaspoon dry ranch seasoning mix
¼ teaspoon paprika
¼ teaspoon Worcestershire sauce

Stir all the ingredients together in a bowl. Store, covered, in a refrigerator and use within 3–4 days. Serve as a dip, salad dressing, or in sandwiches.

Avo-Ranch Dressing

Delicious on Mexican foods, salads, or with scrambled eggs at breakfast. **Makes 1½ cups.**

1 small, ripe avocado
1 cup buttermilk
2 tablespoons lemon juice
1 clove garlic, minced
2 tablespoons chopped fresh dill
1 tablespoon chopped fresh chives
Sea salt and freshly ground black pepper, to taste

Peel and pit the avocado and scoop the flesh into a blender or food processor. Add the buttermilk, lemon juice, and garlic and pulse until well combined. Add the fresh herbs and season to taste.

Cheesy Cilantro Ranch Dressing

With its jalapeño, cilantro, and cheese, this dressing is a
great accompaniment to Mexican salads, tacos, and burritos.
Makes about 1½ cups.

1 cup ranch dressing
2 cloves crushed garlic
½ teaspoon ground cumin
¼ cup chopped fresh cilantro (coriander)
1 tablespoon white wine vinegar
¼ cup grated cheddar cheese
1 jalapeño pepper, chopped

Place all the ingredients in a food processor or blender and
pulse until well combined. Add a little more thinned ranch if
needed to get the desired consistency.

Chipotle Ranch Dressing

Spoon on Mexican food, such as tacos or burritos, or on salads for a smoky flavor. **Makes about 3 cups.**

  2 tablespoons dry ranch seasoning mix
  2½ cups sour cream
  3 tablespoons lime juice
  3 tablespoons chipotle pepper (adobo) puree
  1 teaspoon ground cumin
  2 tablespoons chopped fresh cilantro (coriander)

Mix all the ingredients in a bowl, stirring until well combined. Cover and place in the refrigerator for 30 minutes before serving to allow the flavors to develop.

Ranchamole

Not only is this recipe a great alternative to guacamole with tortilla chips, you can also drizzle it on fish tacos or use it as a dip for chicken wings. **Makes about 1½ cups.**

¼ cup buttermilk
¼ cup sour cream
1 tablespoon white wine vinegar
1 clove garlic, grated
Few dashes of hot sauce
2 tablespoons chopped fresh flat-leaf parsley
2 tablespoons chopped fresh dill
1 tablespoon chopped fresh chives
1 avocado, peeled, pitted, and mashed
Dash of lemon juice
Sea salt and freshly ground black pepper
Tortilla chips, to serve

Mix together the buttermilk, sour cream, white wine vinegar, garlic, hot sauce, parsley, dill, and chives. Add the mashed avocado and lemon juice, then taste and season. Serve with tortilla chips.

Ranch Hummus

Creamy and easy, this makes a great sandwich filler as well as a dip. **Makes about 2 cups.**

1½ cups canned chickpeas
½ cup plain Greek yogurt
1½ tablespoons lemon juice
Freshly ground black pepper
2 tablespoons dry ranch seasoning mix
2 tablespoons water
Sea salt and freshly ground black pepper
Chili flakes (optional)
Vegetable crudités or crackers, to serve

Place the first six ingredients in a food processor and pulse for about 2 minutes until well blended. Add another tablespoon of water to loosen, if needed, and season to taste. Top with chili flakes for an extra bit of heat. Serve with crudités or crackers.

Blue Ranch Dip

Perfect for spicy buffalo wings. **Makes 2 cups.**

¼ cup softened cream cheese
¼ cup mayonnaise
½ cup ranch salad dressing
½ cup sour cream
½ cup crumbled blue cheese
2 tablespoons chopped fresh chives
Sea salt and freshly ground black pepper

Place the first four ingredients in a bowl and blend well until
fully combined. Stir in the chopped chives and season to taste
with salt and pepper.

Blue Buffalo Dip

Serve this hearty dip with tortilla chips, toasted pita bread triangles, or crudités. **Makes about 3 cups.**

    1 cup diced cooked chicken
    ½ cup softened cream cheese
    ¼ cup ranch salad dressing
    ¼ cup blue cheese salad dressing
    ¼ cup crumbled blue cheese
    2 teaspoons hot pepper sauce
    2 tablespoons chopped fresh cilantro (coriander)
        or green onions

Stir the chicken, cream cheese, salad dressings, blue cheese, and hot pepper sauce together in a saucepan over a low heat. Mix well until fully combined and continue to heat gently for about 15 minutes until everything has melted. Stir in the chopped cilantro or green onions and taste, adding more hot pepper sauce if desired. Serve warm.

Variation: Substitute the blue cheese salad dressing for an extra ¼ cup of ranch.

Dry Ranch Seasoning Mix

This dry seasoning can be mixed with milk and mayo for
a salad dressing, used as a seasoning for breadcrumbs
or croutons, or added instead of dried herbs when cooking.

¼ cup dry buttermilk powder
2 tablespoons dried minced onion
2 tablespoons dried parsley
1 tablespoon dried chives
1 teaspoon garlic powder
1 teaspoon dried celery flakes
½ teaspoon white pepper
¼ teaspoon paprika
¼ teaspoon dried dill
Sea salt and freshly ground pepper, to taste

Mix all the ingredients together in a jar with a lid, then close
and store in a cool, dark place. For a finer blend, grind in a
spice grinder or food processor.

Ways to Use Dry Ranch Mix

Sprinkle on potatoes before frying or roasting.

•

Add to breadcrumbs for a seasoned coating for meat.

•

Include in croutons for salads.

•

Sprinkle over fish or meat, pizza or pasta.

•

Use as a general seasoning for savory recipes.

•

Add to soup, stews, chili con carne, or casseroles.

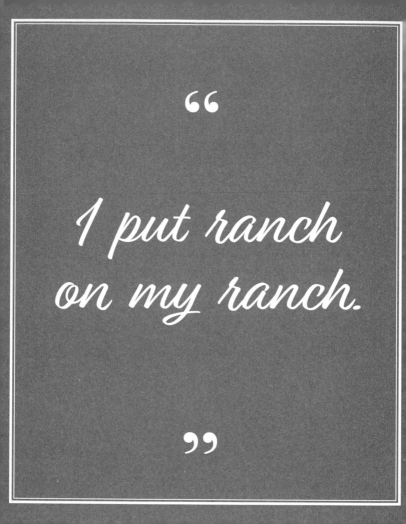

"

I put ranch
on my ranch.

"

Ranch Cheese Spread

Serve with crackers or crudités. **Makes 4 cups.**

  1 cup softened cream cheese
  1 cup soured cream
  ½ cup mayonnaise
  2 cups grated cheese
  2 green onions, chopped
  2 tablespoons dry ranch seasoning mix

Beat the cream cheese, sour cream, and mayonnaise in a bowl
until smooth. Stir in the grated cheese, green onions, and
ranch dressing mix. Refrigerate for at least 30 minutes before
serving to allow the flavors to develop.

Bacon Ranch Dip

Serve with tortilla chips or bread rounds. **Makes 2½ cups.**

1 cup softened cream cheese
½ cup grated cheddar cheese
½ cup grated mozzarella cheese
½ cup sour cream
1 tablespoon dry ranch seasoning mix
4 strips of bacon, cooked and crumbled
1 teaspoon dried oregano
1 tablespoon chopped fresh cilantro (coriander)

Preheat oven to 350°F (180°C/Gas mark 4). Combine all the
ingredients, except the cilantro, in a bowl and stir well.
Transfer the mixture to a small ovenproof dish and bake,
covered, for 30 minutes until heated through and bubbling.
Remove from the oven, garnish with the cilantro, and serve.

ELEVATE YOUR RANCH

Pimp up your store-bought ranch dressing with these flavor combos.

•

Make it herby by adding in chopped fresh dill, chives, and parsley, or a dollop of dill or basil pesto.

•

Amp up with heat by adding a dash of sriracha, Mexican hot pepper sauce, or a spoonful of Moroccan harissa paste.

•

Mix half BBQ sauce and half ranch to make a great chargrilled burger topping.

•

Go Greek by adding finely chopped cucumber to make a tzatziki blend.

•

Adding buffalo wing sauce and blue cheese to your ranch will transform it into a wing dip.

Kicking Cajun Ranch Dipping Sauce

Serve with tortilla chips or as an accompaniment to blackened salmon or shrimp and rice. **Makes 1 cup.**

1 cup ranch dressing, preferably homemade
3 tablespoons Cajun seasoning
¼ teaspoon cayenne pepper

Place all the ingredients in a bowl, stir well to combine, then taste and add more cayenne if necessary. Cover and refrigerate for 1–2 hours to allow the flavors to develop.

Greek Feta Ranch Dip

Serve with toasted pita bread triangles. **Makes 2½ cups.**

    1 cup sour cream
    ¼ cup buttermilk
    ½ cup roughly chopped green onions
    ½ cup feta, crumbled, plus extra for topping
    1 clove minced garlic
    1 teaspoon fresh lemon juice
    2 tablespoons chopped fresh oregano
    ½ teaspoon salt
    2 teaspoons freshly ground black pepper
    Chopped fresh dill and cayenne pepper, to serve

Place all the ingredients in a food processor, except the dill, cayenne, and reserved feta, and process until well blended and creamy. Chill until ready to serve, then top with chopped fresh dill, chopped feta, and a dash of cayenne for color.

"

I'd rather be drinking ranch.

"

Sesame Ranch Dressing

This Asian-influenced ranch is excellent with salads or stir-fries.
Makes 1 cup.

⅓ cup extra-virgin olive oil
2 tablespoons ranch dressing
3 tablespoons rice vinegar
2 tablespoons miso paste
1 tablespoon tahini
2 teaspoons dry ranch seasoning mix
1 teaspoon soy sauce
½ teaspoon toasted sesame oil
Sea salt and freshly ground black pepper

In a blender or food processor, puree the olive oil, vinegar,
miso, tahini, dry ranch seasoning mix, soy sauce, and sesame
oil until smooth. Add a little water if needed. Taste and
season with salt and pepper.

Extra Cool Cucumber Ranch

This pairs well with crispy lettuce, such as iceberg, as well as crudités and corn. **Makes 1½ cups.**

1 cucumber, peeled and diced
¾ cup sour cream
¼ cup mayonnaise
¼ cup buttermilk
2 cloves garlic, minced
Juice and zest of 1 lemon
1 teaspoon honey
2 green onions, sliced
2 tablespoons chopped fresh parsley
2 tablespoons chopped fresh dill
Sea salt and freshly ground pepper

In a blender or food processor, combine the cucumber, sour cream, mayonnaise, buttermilk, garlic, lemon juice and zest, and honey. Process until smooth. Stir in the green onions and herbs, then add salt and pepper to taste.

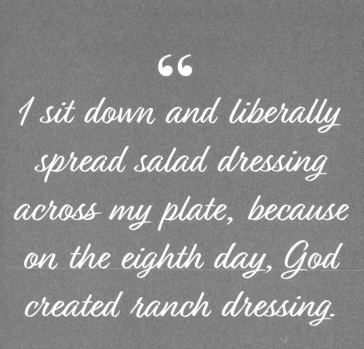

66

I sit down and liberally spread salad dressing across my plate, because on the eighth day, God created ranch dressing.

99

American author Julie Murphy

Loaded Ranch Dip

A meal in itself, this is great served with tortilla chips and crackers. **Makes 2 cups.**

1 cup softened cream cheese
2 tablespoons dry ranch seasoning mix
1 red or green chili pepper, deseeded and chopped
1 red bell pepper, finely diced
¼ cup chopped black olives
¼ cup canned corn
Chopped fresh cilantro (coriander), to garnish

Mix the softened cream cheese with the seasoning and chili until well combined, then stir in the pepper, olives, and corn. Cover and refrigerate to allow the flavors to develop. Sprinkle with the fresh cilantro to serve.

Ranch Butter

A versatile butter to use in mashed potatoes, on roast potatoes, pasta, steamed vegetables, corn on the cob, seafood, or steak.
Makes 1 cup.

1 cup softened butter
1 tablespoon dry ranch seasoning mix
Chopped fresh dill and parsley

Mix the butter and ranch mix to combine, mashing well, then stir in the fresh herbs. You can form this into a log and freeze in sliced rounds to pop into your dishes when cooking.

Chapter Three

Snacks, Salads, & Sides

....

Sizzle up your snacks
with ranch-flavored
pretzels, pumpkin seeds,
popcorn, potato salad,
and coleslaw.

Ranch Pretzels

Transform ordinary mini pretzels into a gourmet snack with ranch seasoning. **Makes 4 cups.**

¼ cup vegetable oil
⅛ teaspoon garlic salt
⅛ teaspoon lemon pepper
¼ teaspoon dried dill
1–2 tablespoons dry ranch seasoning mix
4 cups mini pretzels

Toss everything together and set aside to rest for about 1 hour. Preheat the oven to 275°F (140°C/Gas mark 1). Line a baking sheet with parchment paper.

Place the pretzels on the baking sheet in a single layer and bake for 20 minutes, then remove. Let cool before serving.

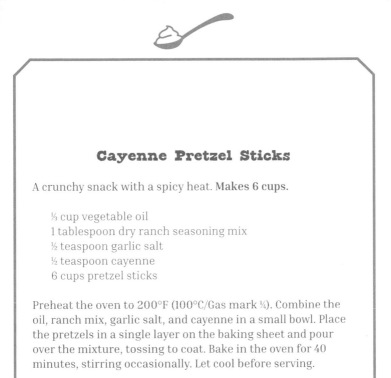

Cayenne Pretzel Sticks

A crunchy snack with a spicy heat. **Makes 6 cups.**

⅓ cup vegetable oil
1 tablespoon dry ranch seasoning mix
½ teaspoon garlic salt
½ teaspoon cayenne
6 cups pretzel sticks

Preheat the oven to 200°F (100°C/Gas mark ¼). Combine the oil, ranch mix, garlic salt, and cayenne in a small bowl. Place the pretzels in a single layer on the baking sheet and pour over the mixture, tossing to coat. Bake in the oven for 40 minutes, stirring occasionally. Let cool before serving.

Ranch-roasted Chickpeas

Irresistible snack food, these chickpeas are crunchy on the outside and soft inside. **Makes 1½ cups.**

1½ cups canned chickpeas
2 teaspoons extra-virgin olive oil
1 tablespoon dry ranch seasoning mix

Preheat the oven to 375°F (190°C/Gas mark 5). Line a baking sheet with parchment paper. Toss the chickpeas with the olive oil and ranch mix. Spread in a single layer on the baking sheet and roast in the oven for 20–25 minutes until golden and crunchy. Let cool before serving.

Ranch Pumpkin Seeds

A crunchy snack that is highly nutritious and packed with powerful antioxidants. It can be spiced up with extra paprika. **Makes 1½ cups.**

1½ cups unsalted roasted pumpkin seeds
1 tablespoon melted butter
1 tablespoon dry ranch seasoning mix
1 teaspoon mustard powder
¼ teaspoon paprika
2 tablespoons grated parmesan cheese
Sea salt, to taste.

Preheat oven to 375°F (190°C/Gas mark 5). Line a baking sheet with parchment paper. Toss the pumpkin seeds in the melted butter, then stir in the ranch seasoning, mustard, paprika, and cheese. Spread in a single layer on the baking sheet and bake for 10 minutes, stirring halfway through. Remove from the heat, let cool, and season with sea salt.

Party Snax Mix

There are many versions of this mix, most of which include breakfast cereal, a crispy corn snack, or mini cheese crackers. Whatever brand you choose, make sure all the ingredients are of similar size. **Makes 6 cups.**

    2 cups corn-rice breakfast cereal
    2 cups mini pretzels
    2 cups mini cheddar cheese crackers
    2 cups cashews
    ¼ cup vegetable oil
    2 tablespoons dry ranch seasoning mix
    ¼ teaspoon garlic powder

Preheat the oven to 275°F (140°C/Gas mark 1). Line a baking sheet with parchment paper. Place the breakfast cereal, pretzels, crackers, and cashews in a bowl. In a separate bowl, whisk together the oil, ranch mix, and garlic powder. Pour over the dry cereal mix and toss well. Arrange in a single layer on the baking sheet and toast in the oven for 15 minutes, stirring halfway through.

RANCH POPCORN

Toss **6** cups of popped popcorn with **2** tablespoons melted butter and sprinkle over **1** tablespoon of ranch seasoning mix. If desired, add **3** tablespoons of grated parmesan cheese. Season to taste with salt and pepper.

The most popular snacking flavors in the U.S. are barbecue, salt, and ranch, according to Food Business News 2020.

Baked Ranch Zucchini Crisps

A healthy herby alternative to potato chips. **Serves 2–4.**

2 zucchini (courgettes), sliced very thinly into rounds
1 tablespoon extra-virgin olive oil
1 tablespoon dry ranch seasoning mix
1 teaspoon dried oregano
Sea salt and freshly ground black pepper

Preheat oven to 225°F (110°C/ Gas mark ¼). Lightly oil a large baking sheet. Pat the zucchini with paper towels to reduce excess moisture and toss with the oil, ranch seasoning, and oregano in a small bowl. Grind over sea salt and black pepper. Place in a single layer on the tray and bake for about 1 hour. Check to see if they are crisping up, and bake for a further 15 minutes if needed. Let cool before serving.

Cool Ranch Tortilla Chips

So much better than the store-bought versions, and no preservatives in sight. **Serves 4–6.**

   10 small corn tortillas
   4 tablespoons dry ranch seasoning mix
   2 teaspoons smoked paprika
   1 teaspoon onion powder
   1 teaspoon garlic powder
   Good grinding of sea salt
   Canola or other vegetable oil for frying

Cut the tortillas into six wedges to make tortilla chips. Mix all the dry seasonings together in a bowl. Set aside.

Heat the oil to 350°F (180°C) in a deep-sided skillet, about 2 inches (5 cm) deep. Fry the tortillas in the oil in batches for about 3 minutes until crispy. If the tortillas puff up, press them down with a wooden spoon. When golden, remove with a slotted spoon and place on a paper towel to drain. While still warm, sprinkle over the seasoning and toss to coat.

CUCUMBER RANCH SALAD

For a healthy, fresh-tasting treat or side salad with a sandwich, sprinkle ranch seasoning mix and a dash of lemon juice over cubed cucumber. Toss, add salt and pepper to taste, and garnish with chopped fresh dill. For a creamy version, substitute ranch dressing for the seasoning mix.

Ranch Bread Sticks

A ranch-seasoned cheesy breadstick for dipping in your ranch hummus (see page 53). **Makes about 10.**

    1 cup grated cheddar cheese
    2 tablespoons dry ranch seasoning mix
    ¼ teaspoon crushed red chilies
    1 egg
    1 sheet frozen puff pastry, thawed

Preheat the oven to 375°F (190°C/Gas mark 5) and line two baking sheets with parchment paper. Mix the cheddar, ranch mix, and chilies together in a bowl. Dust ¼ of the mixture over a work surface.

Lay down one sheet of the puff pastry on top of the cheese mixture and top with another ¼ cup of the seasoned cheese. Roll out the pastry until about ⅛ inch (4 mm) thick, making sure the cheese is pressed into the pastry. Fold in half and repeat with the remaining cheese mixture, rolling again. Slice the pastry into long strips, about 1 inch (2.5 cm) wide. Transfer to the parchment paper, twisting each one along the length. Chill for 10 minutes in the refrigerator before baking for 15 minutes or until golden brown.

Ranch Dill Pickles

Add 2 tablespoons of ranch seasoning mix to a jar of dill pickles, shake well, and refrigerate for 24 hours before eating.

66

According to Statista, U.S. Census data and Simmons' National Consumer Study, 9.16 million Americans used three or more bottles of ranch dressing per month in 2020. 18.5 million used two bottles.

99

Ranch Chicken Mayo

Use this chicken mayo to top salads or as sandwich fillers.
Makes about 4 cups.

- 3 cups shredded cooked chicken
- 1 cup chopped celery
- 1 red bell pepper, finely diced
- ¼ cup chopped red onion
- ½ cup mayonnaise
- 1 tablespoon dry ranch seasoning mix

Mix all the ingredients together in a bowl, stirring well to combine. Cover and chill in the refrigerator for 1 hour to allow the flavors to develop before serving.

Ranch Waldorf Salad

Chop the ingredients in similar bite-size pieces. Choose crisp varieties of green and red apples. **Serves 2.**

2 cups shredded cooked chicken
1 cup diced celery
1 cup diced green apple
1 cup diced red apple
½ cup golden raisins (sultanas)
¼ cup dried cranberries
½ cup ranch salad dressing
1 tablespoon fresh lemon juice
2 cups torn butter lettuce
¼ cup roughly chopped walnuts
Chopped fresh dill, to serve

Toss the chicken, celery, apple, raisins, and cranberries with the ranch dressing and lemon juice. Cover and refrigerate. When ready to serve, divide the lettuce leaves between two plates, and top each with the chilled salad. Toss over the walnuts and fresh dill.

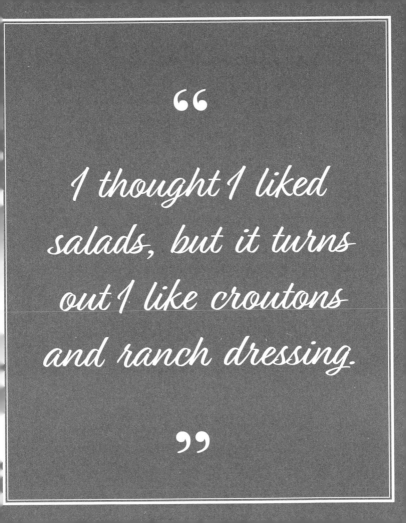

"

I thought I liked salads, but it turns out I like croutons and ranch dressing.

"

Avocado Ranch Salad

A fresh zesty salad for a light lunch. **Serves 2.**

1 small avocado
2 teaspoons fresh lime juice
2 carrots, diced
1 yellow bell pepper, diced
½ red onion, diced
½ cup canned corn
2 tablespoons ranch salad dressing
Sea salt and freshly ground black pepper, to taste

Peel, pit, and dice the avocado. Place in a small bowl and sprinkle over the lime juice. In a serving bowl, add the carrot, pepper, onion, and corn. Add the ranch dressing and stir to combine. Toss in the avocado, season to taste, and serve.

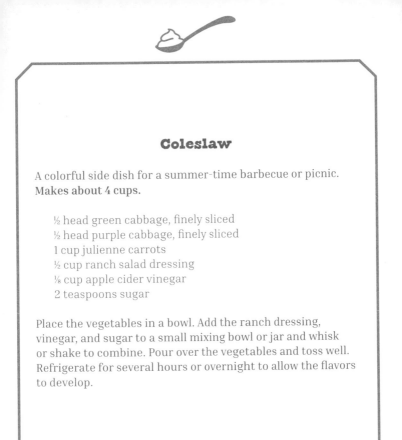

Coleslaw

A colorful side dish for a summer-time barbecue or picnic.
Makes about 4 cups.

½ head green cabbage, finely sliced
½ head purple cabbage, finely sliced
1 cup julienne carrots
½ cup ranch salad dressing
⅛ cup apple cider vinegar
2 teaspoons sugar

Place the vegetables in a bowl. Add the ranch dressing,
vinegar, and sugar to a small mixing bowl or jar and whisk
or shake to combine. Pour over the vegetables and toss well.
Refrigerate for several hours or overnight to allow the flavors
to develop.

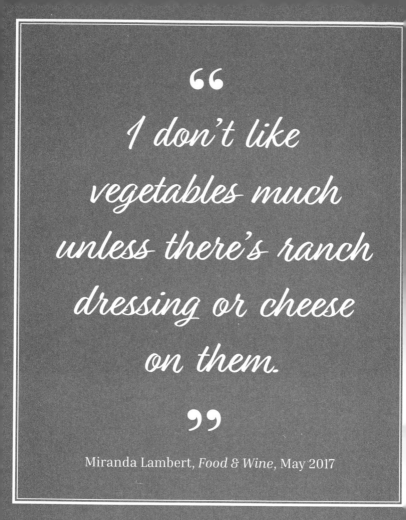

"

I don't like vegetables much unless there's ranch dressing or cheese on them.

"

Miranda Lambert, *Food & Wine*, May 2017

Ranch Green Beans

A tangy side dish to serve with barbecued chicken or grilled steak. **Serves 4.**

4 cups fresh green beans, trimmed
2 tablespoons extra-virgin olive oil
2 tablespoons ranch dressing
1 tablespoon finely chopped green onions
4 slices bacon, cooked and crumbled

Steam or boil the green beans until just tender. Drain and run under cold water, then toss with the olive oil. Add the green beans and ranch dressing to a skillet and sauté over a medium heat until tender. Transfer to a serving bowl, top with the green onions and bacon, and serve.

Glazed Carrots

Flavor an ordinary veggie side dish with ranch and brown sugar. **Serves 4.**

    1 pound (450 g) small carrots, sliced lengthwise
    2 tablespoons butter
    2 tablespoons dry ranch seasoning mix
    2 tablespoons brown sugar

Boil or steam the carrots until they are just tender. Drain. In a saucepan over a low heat, combine the butter, ranch seasoning, and brown sugar. Stir until the sugar has dissolved. Add the carrots, toss to glaze, and serve.

66

1. Open bag of frozen tots.

2. Bake said tots until burnt on outside but kind of still cold inside.

3. Serve with ranch dressing.

Olivia Wilde, Twitter, September 2015

Ranch dressing had a cameo in Amy Schumer's 2018 movie, *I Feel Pretty*, where Amy's character is seen licking the ranch on her fingers. In real life, Amy loves ranch so much that she told Jimmy Fallon her dream food would be "a hero, and I want it to be called 'The Amy Schumer' . . . chicken cutlet, bacon, cheddar, lettuce, tomato, ranch on [. . .] toasted garlic bread."

Bacon Ranch Potato Salad

Picnics and barbecues wouldn't be the same without the obligatory potato salad. **Serves 4.**

4 cups cubed potatoes
¼ cup chopped green onions
8 bacon slices, cooked and crumbled
1⅓ cups mayonnaise
3 tablespoons ranch salad dressing
2 tablespoons Dijon mustard
4 teaspoons white wine vinegar
½ teaspoon minced garlic
3 tablespoons grated parmesan cheese
2 tablespoons chopped fresh flat-leaf parsley
Sea salt and freshly ground pepper, to taste

Place the potatoes in a large saucepan, cover with water, and bring to a boil. Reduce the heat, cover, and simmer for 15 minutes until just tender. Drain and place in a large bowl with the onion and bacon.

Whisk together the mayo, ranch, mustard, vinegar, garlic, and parmesan. Pour over the potatoes, toss well, then add the parsley and season to taste. Refrigerate until ready to serve.

Baked Steak Frites

Robust ranch-flavored fries are a meal in themselves, never mind about the steak. **Serves 4–6.**

    4 large potatoes, such as russet, Yukon gold, or Maris Piper
    ½ cup freshly grated parmesan cheese
    2 tablespoons dry ranch seasoning mix
    ½ teaspoon onion powder
    ½ teaspoon garlic powder
    Sea salt and freshly ground black pepper, to taste
    2 tablespoons extra-virgin olive oil
    3 tablespoons chopped fresh flat-leaf parsley

Preheat the oven to 375°F (190°C/Gas mark 5). Line a baking sheet with aluminum foil or parchment paper. Scrub the potatoes but don't peel, then slice each into 8 thick wedges, cutting lengthwise. Dry with paper towels.

In a large bowl, combine the parmesan, ranch mix, onion powder, garlic powder, salt and pepper, and stir well. Whisk in the olive oil. Add the potato wedges and toss to coat. Tip onto the baking sheet in a single layer and bake for 30 minutes until cooked through. Toss with the fresh herbs and any extra seasoning or cheese, to serve.

"

I eat ranch dressing with my pizza; I dip it in the ranch. It's so good! I know, I am really weird.

"

Jamie Lynn Spears

Chapter Four

Hearty Helpings

....

Marinades, recipes, and
food hacks to add ranch
to casseroles, fried
chicken, grills,
garlic potatoes, eggs,
sandwiches, and more.

RANCH OUT

Use ranch as an all-in-one seasoning, thickening agent, and flavor booster for all types of savory dishes, whether you are stewing, roasting, baking, frying, or sautéing.

Add bottled dressing or dry ranch seasoning mix to burgers, meatloaf, and meatballs for an instant flavor boost.

Mix it into a homemade pan gravy to add richness.

Substitute ranch dressing for half the amount of mayonnaise in your baked casseroles—it can handle the heat plus it adds creaminess.

Add a tablespoon or two of dry ranch seasoning to soups, stews, and chili con carne. Not only does it give a tasty seasoning but also helps thicken the dish.

Sprinkle over roast beef or lamb shanks before slow-cooking or add it to stockpot dishes.

Elevate a cream or cheese sauce by adding in ranch dressing or dry mix, or use ranch to boost the flavor of a roux or béchamel sauce.

Use the dressing as a pizza base sauce instead of tomato sauce.

Combine dry ranch mix with olive oil and use in dressings, marinades, or to roast potatoes or vegetables.

Combine ranch with butter for finishing off steamed vegetables, fish, or steak.

Add the dry mix to a store-bought veggie tomato sauce for pasta or a meat-based ragu for spaghetti Bolognese or lasagne.

Substitute ranch dressing for half the mayonnaise in your tuna, chicken, or ham salad.

Stir a tablespoon or two of dry mix into your rice while it's cooking, or into your stir-fry.

Meat Marinade

Pour the bottled dressing over chicken and let it sit for at least 30 minutes before cooking. Or combine a packet of dry ranch seasoning mix with olive oil, vinegar, mustard, and Worcestershire sauce for a marinade you can use on grilled chicken, pork, fish, and vegetables.

Lemon-garlic Chicken Marinade

For deep flavors that tenderize and work really well with meat on a barbecue grill, use this marinate overnight. **Serves 4.**

1½ cups ranch dressing
Juice and zest of 1 lemon
2 cloves garlic, minced
¼ cup extra-virgin olive oil
Sea salt and freshly ground black pepper
2 tablespoons chopped fresh tarragon
4 chicken breasts

In a food processor or blender, combine the ranch, lemon zest and juice, garlic, olive oil, salt and pepper. Process until well blended. Stir in the tarragon.

Place the chicken in a large freezer bag and pour over the marinade to coat well. Close the bag tightly and refrigerate overnight. The next day, fire up your grill to a medium heat and cook the chicken breasts slowly for about 25 minutes, turning once.

Scrambled Eggs Ranch-Style

The secret to these eggs is using buttermilk instead of regular cow's milk. **Serves 2–4.**

    2 tablespoons dry ranch seasoning mix
    4 tablespoons buttermilk
    6 large eggs
    1 tablespoon butter
    Sea salt and freshly ground black pepper, to taste
    Chopped fresh chives, to garnish

In a bowl, whisk together the ranch seasoning and buttermilk until airy, then add in the eggs and whisk until frothy. Heat the butter in a skillet, swirling to cover the base, and add in the egg mixture. Stir constantly with a wooden spoon, or whisk if you want very fluffy eggs. When the eggs are just cooked but still shiny, remove from the heat, add salt and pepper to taste, sprinkle over the chives, and serve.

Ranchified Breakfasts

Add ranch seasoning to your hollandaise sauce
when making eggs Benedict or eggs Florentine.

•

Sprinkle ranch seasoning over your
omelette just as it is setting.

•

Top your avocado toast with dry ranch seasoning
mixed with crushed ancho chilies, or swirl a little
ranch dressing into the mashed avocado.

•

Drizzle ranch dressing over your breakfast burrito.

•

Fry up home-fry potatoes with ranch seasoning or
put it into your hash browns.

The Saucy Sauce

No more need to decide between the two most popular sauces: A holy grail combination of ketchup and ranch dressing, called Kranch, was launched by Heinz in 2019.

Chipotle Ranch Sandwich Spread

Excellent in a turkey sandwich or taco. **Makes about 1½ cups.**

    1 cup sour cream
    ½ cup mayonnaise
    2 tablespoons dry ranch seasoning mix
    1 teaspoon apple cider vinegar
    1 tablespoon whole milk
    2 canned chipotle peppers, finely chopped
    2 teaspoons adobo sauce

Mix all the ingredients together in a small bowl, then cover
and chill for 3–4 hours until the flavors have developed. Use
instead of mayo in sandwiches, heroes, pitas, tacos, burgers,
and other sandwiches.

Ranch Grilled Cheese

An extra creamy toasted cheese sandwich made with cream cheese and ranch. **Makes 4.**

⅔ cup softened cream cheese
⅔ cup mayonnaise
1 cup grated cheddar cheese
1 cup grated Monterey jack cheese (or substitute havarti)
1 tablespoon dry ranch seasoning mix
8 slices sourdough bread
4 tablespoons butter

Beat the cream cheese and mayo together until combined and smooth, then stir in the cheese and ranch mix. Place the bread on a work surface and butter one side of each piece. Divide the mixture between 6 slices on the unbuttered side and cover with the other slices. The buttered sides will be on the outside of the sandwich. Fry in a skillet over a medium heat until the cheese has melted and the bread is golden. Serve immediately.

Ranch Breadcrumbs

The ranch mix adds an instant herby onion flavor to ordinary breadcrumbs. **Makes 2 cups.**

1 tablespoon dry ranch seasoning mix
2 cups panko breadcrumbs
1½ teaspoons dried parsley
1½ teaspoons dried oregano
1½ teaspoons dried dill

Combine the ranch seasoning with panko breadcrumbs, parsley, dill, and oregano. Use the mixture for coating mozzarella sticks, veal escalopes, schnitzel, or chicken goujons by dipping in flour, then buttermilk or egg, and then dipping in the breadcrumbs to coat before frying or baking.

Grilled Ranch Potatoes

A great outdoor side dish for a summer BBQ, or cook under your broiler. **Serves 6.**

2 pounds (1 kg) baby potatoes, halved
¼ tablespoon extra-virgin olive oil
Juice of ½ a lemon
1–2 tablespoons dry ranch seasoning mix
Sea salt and freshly ground black pepper
Ranch dressing, for drizzling
Chopped fresh chives

Preheat a barbecue grill or broiler to a medium heat. In a large bowl, toss the potatoes with olive oil, lemon juice, and ranch seasoning. Season with salt and pepper. Thread potatoes onto skewers and grill until tender, about 20 minutes, taking care not to burn them. Drizzle with ranch dressing, garnish with chives, and serve.

Tip: If your potatoes are on the larger size, parboil them for a couple minutes first.

66

The baseline for ranch needs to be the packet of buttermilk Hidden Valley. Emphasis on buttermilk and emphasis on packet. Bottle is trash, dip is trash.

99

Chrissy Teigen, on her ranch dressing rule, Twitter, May 2018

Herby Ranch Skewers

A quick chicken skewer for the barbecue grill. **Serves 6.**

½ cup extra-virgin olive oil
½ cup ranch dressing
1 tablespoon chopped fresh rosemary
Juice and zest of ½ lemon
1 teaspoon white wine vinegar
1 tablespoon honey
Sea salt and freshly ground black pepper
5 chicken breasts, cut into 1-inch (2.5-cm) cubes
Red bell pepper, cut into chunks

Combine all the ingredients except the chicken and bell pepper in a large bowl and stir together to combine. Place the cubed chicken and bell pepper in the bowl and toss to coat. Cover and refrigerate for at least 1 hour. Preheat a broiler or barbecue grill to a medium heat. Thread the chicken and peppers onto skewers and cook for 10–15 minutes, turning once, until cooked through and lightly charred.

Ranch dressing appears on 26 percent of menus in the U.S., according to Food Genius.
66 percent of menus that mention ranch pair it with chicken.

Cocktail Meatballs

Serve these as tasty cocktail snacks for parties. Alternatively they make a hearty meal with mashed potatoes and gravy, Swedish style, or add them to a tomato pasta sauce and served with spaghetti. **Makes about 25.**

1 pound (450 kg) ground beef
1 egg, lightly beaten
2 tablespoons milk
½ cup plain breadcrumbs
1 tablespoon dry ranch seasoning mix
¼ teaspoon oregano
Ranch dip, to serve (optional)

Preheat the oven to 350°F (180°C/Gas mark 4). Lightly oil a shallow baking tray or ovenproof dish. In a medium bowl, combine all the ingredients except the dip and stir to mix well, but do not overwork. Shape into meatballs and place in the dish. Bake for 20–25 minutes until browned and serve with ranch dip.

Ranch Potato Skins

A snack favorite, these make a substantial lunch when served with a green salad. **Serves 2.**

2 baking potatoes
Sea salt
1 tablespoon dry ranch seasoning mix
¼ cup ranch dressing
¼ cup grated mozzarella cheese
¼ cup grated cheddar cheese
4 slices bacon, cooked and crispy
Chopped fresh chives and ranch dressing, to serve

Preheat the oven to 350°F (180°C/Gas mark 4). Wash the potatoes thoroughly. Rub the skins with salt, poke a couple holes in each with a knife, and wrap each in foil. Place in the oven and bake for 1–2 hours, depending on their size.

When soft and cooked, slice in half and scoop out a little of the potato flesh, just enough to leave space for the cheese. Top each with the cheese and bacon, drizzle over the ranch, and return to the oven for 15 minutes, until the cheese has melted. Sprinkle over the chives and serve with extra ranch dressing.

Ranch Rice

Dress up ordinary steamed rice with ranch—instead of a medium grain, you could choose basmati, sticky jasmine, or nutty brown rice. **Serves 2.**

 1 cup medium-grain white rice
 2 tablespoons dry ranch seasoning mix
 1 tablespoon butter
 2 cups water

In a medium saucepan, combine rice, dry ranch mix, butter, and water. Heat over medium-high heat until it comes to a full boil. Cover and reduce to low until just simmering and cook for 15–20 minutes, or as according to the packet instructions. Remove from the heat, fluff with a fork, and cover again. Let stand for 5 minutes before serving.

Veggie Mexican Rice Bowl

To the Ranch Rice recipe opposite, add
chopped tomatoes, thinly sliced red onions,
black beans, canned corn kernels, sliced
fresh avocado, a few sliced black olives, slices
fresh red chili, and chopped fresh cilantro
(coriander). Serve with a squeeze of fresh lime
and chipotle ranch dressing (see page 51).

Baked Ranch Salmon

Yes, ranch goes with fish too! Here's an easy weekday meal.
Serves 4.

4 salmon fillets
Juice and zest of 1 lemon
Sea salt and freshly ground black pepper
1 tablespoon chopped fresh tarragon
1 tablespoon chopped fresh dill
⅓ cup ranch dressing

Preheat the oven to 375°F (190°C/Gas mark 5). Line a baking
sheet with foil. Rinse the salmon fillets and pat dry. Mix the
lemon juice and zest, herbs, and salt and pepper in a large
shallow bowl and toss in the salmon to coat. Transfer to the
baking sheet, skin side down, and top each with an even layer
of ranch dressing. Bake for 10 minutes, then place under a
hot grill and broil until the dressing is bubbling and coloring
up. Serve immediately.

Ranch Butter Shrimp

Serve with rice, noodles, or add to a stir-fry. For extra zing, add minced garlic and a squeeze of lemon juice. **Serves 4.**

  1 pound (450 g) raw jumbo shrimp (tiger prawns), peeled
     and deveined
  ½ cup butter
  1 tablespoon dry ranch seasoning mix
  Chopped fresh flat-leaf parsley, to serve

Preheat the oven to 400°F (200°C/Gas mark 6). Place the shrimp on a baking sheet, add the butter, sprinkle over the ranch dressing, and bake for 10 minutes until the shrimp are pink. Garnish with the parsley to serve.

8 percent of Americans put ranch dressing on burgers, **36 percent** think cold pizza dipped in ranch sounds good, and **20 percent** have mixed ranch with salsa.

The Chicago Tribune ranked the best ranch dressings and put Hidden Valley at No.1. However, a separate ranking by "professional" taste testers claimed Ken's ranch dressing was better for dipping.

Quick Chicken Wings

The snack that's a meal. Wings can be barbecued, deep-fried, smoked, or baked, and take on endless flavor combinations. Just don't forget the ranch! **Serves 6–8.**

3 pounds (1½ kg) frozen chicken wings,
   thawed and drained
2 tablespoons olive oil
2 tablespoons dry ranch seasoning mix
1 teaspoon cayenne
Sea salt and freshly ground black pepper
Ranch dressing, to serve

Preheat the oven to 425°F (200°C/Gas mark 6). Line two baking sheets with foil, and lightly oil. In a large bowl, toss the chicken wings with the olive oil to coat, then stir in the ranch dressing mix, cayenne, and salt and pepper. Place the wings on the baking sheets and bake for 20 minutes, then turn and bake for 20 minutes more.

According to Superbowl Sunday statistics gathered by Premio Foods, chopped vegetables with ranch dressing are a popular option for game day and over half of Americans who eat chicken wings prefer to dip them in ranch.

Ranch Mac-and-cheese

This is a quick and easy version, but you can use your own favorite mac-and-cheese recipe, just substitute the ranch mix for your usual dried herbs. **Serves 6.**

4 cups elbow macaroni pasta
4 tablespoons unsalted butter
4 tablespoons all-purpose (plain) flour
3 cups whole milk
2 tablespoons dry ranch seasoning mix
2 cups grated cheddar cheese
Sea salt and freshly ground black pepper

Cook the pasta according to the packet instructions and drain. Heat the butter in a saucepan over a medium heat, until it foams, and then whisk in the flour, bit by bit, until incorporated and smooth. Then slowly add in the milk, whisking all the time, until thickened. Stir in the ranch dressing, and continue to cook for about five minutes more. Remove from the heat, stir in the cheese until melted, and then add the cooked pasta. Season to taste and serve.

Ranch Pasta Salad

Serve this colorful pasta dish as a light lunch or add grilled ranch chicken for a more substantial meal. **Serves 4.**

    2 cups tricolor fusilli pasta shapes
    1 cup chopped broccoli
    1 cup chopped cucumber
    1 cup chopped tomato
    ½ cup grated parmesan cheese
    1¼ cups ranch dressing
    Sea salt and freshly ground pepper

Cook the pasta according to the packet instructions, then drain and rinse under cold water. In a bowl, combine the pasta, broccoli, cucumber, tomatoes, and cheese. Stir to mix well, then add in the ranch dressing, stirring to coat. Adjust seasoning to taste, and eat immediately, or cover and refrigerate until ready to serve.

Chapter Five

Ranch & . . .

Surprising and weird combo ideas for those who dare take their ranch experience to the next level.

AVOCADO TOAST

Ever noticed how well ranch dressing goes with avocado in a salad? You can take it up a gear by pairing it with another favorite—avocado toast. Simply drizzle it over your choice of avo toast recipe, or mash it in with the avocado if you prefer it that way.

Scrambled Eggs and Ranch

The best scrambled eggs is a matter of opinion: Some people prefer them barely cooked and runny, others would rather eat them well cooked. And the jury's out whether heavy cream or sour cream are better. But next time you crack open some eggs for scrambling, try adding a healthy drizzle of ranch dressing.

Ranch and Carbs

There are various recipes that combine rice- or corn-based cereals with pretzel twists, bite-size crackers, and grated parmesan cheese, all seasoned and mixed together with a packet of ranch dressing mix—perfect as a snack food for a party.

Ranch and Cereal

So how about a bowl of cereal with milk and ranch dressing? It has been tried, and reportedly it does work with a cinnamon-flavored cereal. According to Wil Fulton of Thrillist, it wasn't "gross," but it was "different." Wil claims the theory:

$$\text{Ranch} + \text{food} = \text{deliciousness}^2$$

66

Customer: Can you bring us some ranch dressing?

Waiter: How much do you need?

Customer: How much do you have?

Waiter: Say no more.

99

Pancakes and Ranch

Think about it: There are buttermilk pancakes, and ranch dressing's most important ingredient is buttermilk, so why not add ranch dressing to your pancakes? Simply substitute some of the sugar—3–4 tablespoons—for dry ranch dressing mix. If making your own pancakes is too much work, simply pour a little dressing from a bottle, along with the maple syrup, over your pancakes.

Franch Fries

Not everyone automatically chooses ketchup
for fries. Some prefer mayo with fries and
others prefer gravy, so it is easy to see that
dipping fries into ranch dressing would be a
pleasing combination. The next time you make
homemade fries, soak the cut potatoes in milk
then coat them in a dry ranch dressing mix
before frying them.

Ranch and Cheese Puffs

Ranch dressing, of course, is a popular dip for potato chips, tortilla chips, and vegetables, but other snack foods are just as delicious dipped in the dressing. The next time you are snacking on cheese puffs, dip them in ranch dressing—we're positive that you'll think it's a win-win combination.

Grilled Cheese and Ranch

Are you one of those people who likes to dip their grilled cheese sandwich in a condiment? Next time, instead of pouring ketchup or BBQ sauce into a bowl for dipping, use ranch dressing. Alternatively, substitute the butter spread on the bread before grilling the sandwich with ranch.

TURN DOWN THE MEXICAN HEAT

Mexican food, whether a mild quesadilla or a spicy burrito, can benefit from the cool, tangy taste provided by ranch dressing. Simply add a tablespoon or two (or three) of the dressing on top of the filling. You could also mix ranch dressing with an equal quantity of BBQ sauce.

Tangy Dogs

Can't choose between mustard or ketchup for
your hotdog? Reach for ranch to drizzle on top.
Not enough ranch dressing for you? Rather
than topping your dog with sauerkraut, mix
ranch dressing into coleslaw—one part mayo to
one part ranch—and smother your frankfurter
with slaw instead.

Rice with Ranch

Rice as a side can be somewhat bland, but it doesn't have to be. Adding a packet of ranch dressing mix is the perfect way to give a little tang. It works well as a side dish for poultry, but you could also make it a one-pot meal by cooking the rice and ranch with chicken pieces and broccoli florets.

On Top of Spaghetti

You'll either love it or hate it, but there are plenty of recipes online for making spaghetti (and meatballs) with ranch dressing, as well as cold pasta salads. One version includes the dry ranch dressing mix added to a carbonara sauce; in another, the seasoning is mixed into a marinara sauce. Why not try both and decide which is best?

Buffalo Popcorn and . . .

Perhaps you thought sprinkling some dry ranch
seasoning mix into melted butter to toss your
popcorn in would be a good idea—and it is.
But you could take it one step further by also
pouring in some spicy buffalo sauce.
Butter, ranch, and spicy sauce make the perfect
seasoning for popcorn in front of the TV, as long
as you also hand out some napkins.

BBQ RIBS

You've already tried some chicken wings dipped in ranch dressing, so it makes sense to also try drizzling ranch dressing over a rack of spareribs. We're confident that you'll agree: The sweetness of the BBQ sauce and tanginess of the ranch dressing are a perfect pairing.

Sip Ranch Soup

A bowl of tomato, broccoli, or carrot soup really benefits from a ranch-flavored cream to dollop on top—you get that wonderful hot with cold sensation. All you need to do is whip 1–2 tablespoons of dry ranch dressing mix with 1 cup of heavy cream. What could be simpler?

RANCH AND PIZZA, WITH A TWIST

Plenty of people enjoy dipping their pizza into ranch dressing, so much so that pizza chains now sell the combination together. But you don't need to dip—instead, bake the pizza crust with the ranch dressing in it. After you shape the pizza dough, simply sprinkle dry ranch dressing mix all over the top—half a packet should do. Then add your normal toppings.

66

*They came with
unlimited ranch
dressing.*

99

The Good Place, "Most Improved Player"
(series 1, episode 8)

Roasted Turkey, Ranch Style

What would Thanksgiving dinner be without turkey, but you could surprise your guests by making your turkey a little different. Prepare your bird as you would normally do, but season it by mixing together 1 cup of butter with two packets of dry ranch seasoning mix and spreading it over your butterball for a delectable tangy flavor.

Ranch and Watermelon

It's not surprising that ranch dressing makes the perfect dip for vegetables, such as carrot sticks or red pepper strips, but fruit? If you think about it, yogurt and fruit work well together, so changing things up a bit by swapping the yogurt for ranch dressing is only a step away. The real stretch of the imagination, however, comes with a more unusual pairing: watermelon chunks dipped in ranch dressing. Try it and see!

AS AMERICAN AS APPLE PIE

Of course, apple pie is America's favorite, and while some people prefer it naked, for others, the jury's out on what best to serve it with: vanilla ice cream, whipped cream, or fancy crème frâiche. But there is another unusual alternative—make up ranch-flavored whipped cream (see page 146). Or just drizzle some ranch on top, straight from the bottle.

Cookie Dippers

Ice cream manufacturers add cookies to their concoctions, such as chocolate chip cookies and Oreos. If you'd rather not have a cold dessert, dip your cookies into ranch—plain ones would probably work better than those with a lot of flavors or spices.

Hot Chocolate and Ranch?

You've had hot chocolate with marshmallows and hot chocolate with whipped cream on top. But would whipped cream seasoned with ranch dressing mix (see page 146) work, or a little dressing from a bottled blended with the milk? We don't know, but you could experiment if you dare.

"

I love you more
than ranch dressing
(so that's saying a lot).

"

Ranch Dressing Fountain

For those who love ranch dressing on everything, there could not be a perfect wedding celebration without ranch—and now they can even order a ranch dressing fountain, a take on the more usual chocolate fountain, for guests to enjoy. Just make sure there are plenty of things for dipping: carrots, celery, strawberries . . . but perhaps not the wedding cake.

A SHOT OF WHISKEY

We wouldn't recommend doing shots, but you could try adding a spoonful of ranch dressing to a whiskey over ice in an old-fashioned glass for sipping on a cold winter's night. Is it that much different from a popular Irish whiskey brand sold mixed with cream? One reviewer has described it as being "the chaser of the gods."

When to Say "No" to Ranch

Sadly, ranch dressing doesn't work with everything. When experimenting on your own, here are some pointers.

If it already has a sharp flavor, such as key lime pie, the pairing will probably clash.

●

If it has an artificial flavor, such as one you might experience in a pop tart, the ranch dressing could bring out that artificial taste, which isn't the most desirable result.

●

If there are already a lot of elements involved, such as in s'mores, adding ranch dressing could be a step too far.

●

No one seems to like ranch dressing with sushi —take our word for it.

Chapter Six

The Ranch
Fan Club

....

Legions of ranch lovers
can't be wrong. Here are the
plaudits and pairings from
superfan celebrities, chefs,
and influencers across TV,
film, and social media.

"You either love it, or you REALLY love it."

Hidden Valley Ranch

"I'm not a normal person with normal tastebuds, so I'll save you all from cringing/dissing on my late-night flavor pairings, but I will say when I was a kid, with little to no access to anything but my mother's pantry, I'd dip everything in ranch dressing."

Christina Tosi,
American chef and TV personality

Celebrities adore ranch dressing. Chrissy Teigen posts about it on Instagram. Olivia Wilde eats it with tater tots. Katie Perry requests it backstage. Courtney Cox drank it from a bowl on Anderson Cooper's show in 2014, and Melissa McCarthy chugged it in an SNL sketch in 2017 with her slogan "That's good to the last drop".

Heralded as

the greatest American condiment of all time,

ranch may be considered lowbrow or, as *The Washington Post* said in 2016, "extravagant and trashy," but it is a $1 billion industry that surpasses ketchup sales in the U.S.

Salmon with a Side

At the end of a day of playing cards at the World Series of Poker, professional poker player Phil Hellmuth has a routine that he likes to follow.

He always orders poached salmon with mushrooms with a side of ranch dressing to dip his fish in.

"Spaghetti is good with ranch, and spaghetti is good with sugar. You put all of that together and make a sandwich out of it, and you get greatness. People shouldn't judge unless they try it."

Terry Rozier,
professional American basketball player

"It must be the ranch dressing."

Daphne Moon tells Frasier in the titular hit TV comedy series, after sniffing her arm.

Frasier, "I Hate Frasier Crane" (season 1, episode 4)

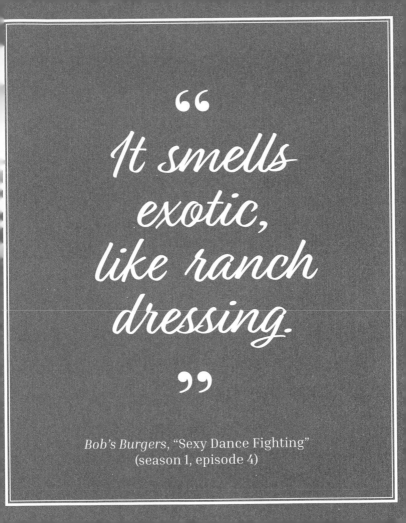

"

It smells exotic, like ranch dressing.

"

Bob's Burgers, "Sexy Dance Fighting"
(season 1, episode 4)

GET OUT THE ONESIE

Here's another vote for ranch and pizza. For **Italia Ricci, the actress known for portraying the Chief of Staff in** *Designated Survivor,* the ideal way to spend an afternoon with nothing to do is to put on a onesie, search Netflix for "a really dark, uncomfortable documentary," and **order a pizza that comes with plenty of ranch dressing as a side.**

Wear the Dressing

We don't mean by spilling it on yourself.
Ranch dressing has become so popular that
it's entered the fashion trade. There are
plenty of T-shirts and sweatshirts with bold
statements and images related to ranch.
And you can even find earrings designed
with pizza slices and a bottle of ranch
dangling in close harmony.

"

I'm serious. You should put ranch dressing on it.

"

Glee, "Britney/Brittany"
(season 2, episode 2)

"There's pork in there, too. See, I rolled it in ranch dressing and then I force-fed it to her."

Master Shake, *Aqua Teen Hunger Force*,
"Revenge of the Trees" (season 2, episode 13)

8 Things Every Ranch Fan Knows

1. **It's not a condiment.**
   A rub, a marinade, a drink, a topping, a dip;
   dry or bottled, it defies categorization.

2. **Not all ranch dressings are equal.**
   Hidden Valley's is thicker and peppier than
   most, but some are distinctly chemical and
   others watery, so get to know your brands.

3. **It's an antidote to spicy.**
   Like a glass of milk with curry, but better.
   Much better.

4. **It's even better spicy.**
Add a dash of tabasco or some sriracha.
You're welcome.

5. **Ask for extra.**
No restaurant ever gives you enough.
Ask for two servings, or four, or six . . .

6. **Keep it stocked in the storecupboard.**
The dry seasoning mix is the only spice
you need; it adds flavor to everything.

7. **All foods are just a delivery system for
ranch.** Veggies, meat, snacks, pizza, and
pasta—they are all just a way to get ranch
into your mouth.

8. **Ranch is a pop culture icon.**
It jumped into the zeitgeist during the
1990s but never stopped making itself
noticed—on TV, in the movies, in music,
and on social media.

Homer's Hose

Ranch dressing has even entered the world of cartoons. In one episode of *The Simpsons*, after America's favorite yellow character loses consciousness from carbon-monoxide fumes, Homer Simpson dreams that he is a sultan accompanied by dancing girls. As he reclines on some large cushions, Homer says: "Enough! I grow weary of your sexually suggestive dancing. Bring me my ranch dressing hose!" As a geyser of ranch dressing is directed into his mouth, Homer's dream-come-true ends, with a camel nudging Homer and calling his name, which turns out to be Ned Flanders' voice waking him up.

Not in the Diet

Staying in shape is important to Colton Haynes, the actor and model who's starred in the TV shows *Teen Wolf* and *Arrow*. He believes his diet plays a 75–80 percent role in keeping fit, and an essential part of it is cutting back on the carbs. **He explains: "I'm from Kansas, so I love ranch dressing and McDonald's. When I'm working, I have to stay away from all that!"**

"I thought that if it looked like ranch dressing ..."

Pretty Little Liars, "Mystery"
(season 2, episode 16)

Brooklyn Nine-Nine

One of America's most popular crime TV shows
seems to have an obsession with ranch dressing.
Here are a few lines from different episodes:

"Just between us, we're nearly out of ranch dressing."

(series 3, episode 13)

"Yeah, I spilled ranch dressing all over the drawer."

(series 4, episode 11)

"They got into a fight over the ranch dressing."

(series 4, episode 20)

SELLING WELL

Ranch dressing is big business. In 2015, Hidden Valley Ranch sold $440 million of the dressing (and that figure doesn't include its competitors). The dressing is particularly popular in the South and Midwest, the areas that make the most sales.

The average American uses ranch dressing on salads 15 times a year,

but who knows how much goes on other food types, such as pizza, hotdogs, fries, chips . . .

> "
>
> *Midwestern kids aren't born. They emerge from corn fields craving ranch dressing.*
>
> "

$1,000 for a Bottle

The owner of Cane Rosso Deep Ellum Pizzeria in Dallas, Texas, was given a bottle of ranch dressing on the pizzeria's opening night. The restaurant has never served ranch dressing to its customers, but the owner, Jay Jerrier, did display the bottle on a wall with a sign reading:

"Side of Delicious Ranch Dressing $1,000.00."

It was eventually purchased, with the money donated to an animal rescue center.

BEDAZZLED BOTTLE

The *Vanderpump Rules* star
Stassi Schroeder was happy to let
Instagram know she had a bedazzled
bottle of Hidden Valley Ranch. The
reality star thinks that people in the
past "didn't want to order ranch at
a restaurant in public," because "it
wasn't considered classy." But as she
explains, the millennials think "this
tastes like heaven, so I don't care."

Get Your Dog in on the Act

One dog-toy manufacturer has produced a toy salad set with the word "Ranch" for dogs to chew on, available at a large pet store retailer. It's even appeared on an Instagram account owned by Charlie, a mini goldendoodle, who had 45,000 followers in 2019. But don't try feeding real ranch dressing to your dog—it's not good for their health.

"Is it weird that I like ranch dressing with everything? I guess that makes my dinner not as healthy :-(it's so yummy with an artichoke."

Kim Kardashian, Twitter, July 2010

RANCH IN A BARREL

For people who put ranch dressing on everything, Hidden Valley introduced a keg filled with their ranch dressing in 2017. It's lined with a special coating to keep the 1⅓ gallons (5 liters) of dressing fresh for as long as it takes to empty the barrel. The company considered it "a year's worth" of dressing. And in case one keg isn't enough, they are stackable.

It's Ranch Day!

That's right, there is a special day on the calendar to celebrate ranch dressing. Make a note on your calendar that **on March 10 you must enjoy as much ranch dressing as you can stomach** to celebrate the existence of the creamy, tangy condiment.

"

Most things can be improved by one of five things: Cheese, BBQ sauce, melted butter, ranch dressing, or chocolate.

"

"Eric: Dude, why do you have so much ranch dressing?

Bullwinkle: Uh, because it's DELICIOUS?"

Hawaii Five-O, "Kapu (Forbidden)",
(season 3, episode 12)

On the School's Menu

Former First Lady Michelle Obama

has spoken out to encourage healthier eating in children, and the U.S. Department of Agriculture (USDA) revised the menus served in schools in 2012. Twice the amount of fruit and vegetables is now offered to the kids, and to help get them to eat those veggies, a low-fat ranch dip can be served with them.

"I love burgers and fries, you know? And I love ice cream and cake. So do most kids. We're not talking about a lifestyle that excludes all that. That's the fun of being a kid. That's the fun of being a human."

First Lady Michelle Obama

RAMSAY USES RANCH

Okay, we're not talking about the chef Gordon Ramsay, known for his use of expletives on television and ability to shout, but **Guy Ramsay Fieri, the American restaurateur and TV presenter known for hosting the Food Network.** Guy posted a salad recipe with homemade ranch dressing, which had an impressive 1.8 million views on TikTok.

The Original

Steve Henson may have created ranch as we know it, but he didn't create the first buttermilk dressing. Recipes for the dressing can be found in Texas dating from 1937, where buttermilk was easier to come by than vegetable oils. Cowboys have probably been enjoying buttermilk dressing for longer than anyone else.

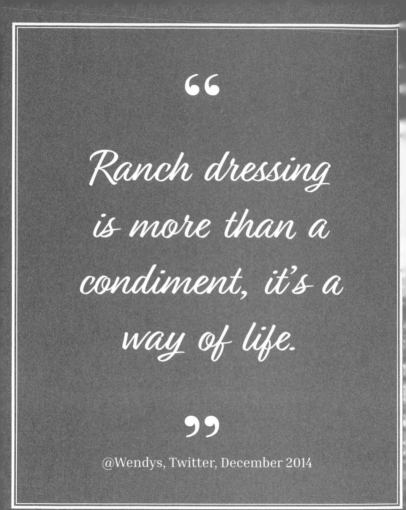

" "

Ranch dressing is more than a condiment, it's a way of life.

" "

@Wendys, Twitter, December 2014